Stewardship Revolution: 30 Days to Take Control of Your Finances God's Way

Bruce Philip Proc Jr

Arise & Shine Transformational Services, LLC

Copyright © 2024 Bruce Proc Jr, Arise & Shine Transformational Services, LLC

All Rights Reserved.

No part of this publication may be reproduced, distributed, or transmitted in any form or by any means, including photocopying, recording, or other electronic or mechanical methods, without the prior written permission of the publisher, except in the case of brief quotations embodied in critical reviews and certain other noncommercial uses permitted by copyright law.

Stewardship Revolution: 30 Days to Take Control of Your Finances God's Way

Table of Contents:

Dedication
Introduction
Day 1: God Owns it All
Day 2: Faithful Stewardship
Day 3: Breaking Free from Debt
Day 4: The Dangers of Loving Money
Day 5: Contentment in Christ
Day 6: Budgeting with Wisdom
Day 7: Trusting God in your Finances
Day 8: Avoid Impulse Spending
Day 9: Saving for the Future
Day 10: Giving Generously
Day 11: The Power of Prayer in Finances
Day 12: The Blessing of Work
Day 13: Handling Financial Temptations
Day 14: God's Provisions in Times of Need
Day 15: Living Below your Means
Day 16: Avoiding the Love of Money
Day 17: Financial Peace Through Giving
Day 18: Planning for Financial Security
Day 19: Debt as a Burden
Day 20: Honoring God with your Wealth
Day 21: Focusing on Eternal Investments
Day 22: Practicing Patience with Finances
Day 23: Living Generously
Day 24: Trusting God with Future Provisions
Day 25: The Power of Contentment
Day 26: The Role of Saving
Day 27: Generosity and Blessing Others
Day 28: Seeking God's Guidance in Financial Decisions
Day 29: Overcoming the Trap of Materialism
Day 30: Faithful Stewardship of All Resources
Day 31 Bonus Devotional
Conclusion: Final Thoughts
Outline for Debt management, Savings, and Resources

Dedication

To my beloved wife, Ashlie, whose unwavering support, encouragement, and love have been a constant source of strength throughout this journey. Your faith and patience have been a guiding light, and I am deeply grateful for your partnership in every aspect of life, especially in this journey toward financial freedom.

To my precious daughter, Adrianna, whose presence fills our home with joy and whose resilience and grace inspire me to be a better man, husband, and father. Your love and understanding have meant more than words can express, and it's with you in mind that I strive to create a better future for us all.

All praise and honor be to Christ Jesus, the ultimate provider, who has shown me that with Him, nothing is impossible. His grace, guidance, and strength are the foundation of this journey, and to Him alone be the glory.

Stewardship Revolution: 30 Days to Take Control of Your Finances God's Way

Introduction: My Journey to Financial Stewardship and Freedom

The journey to getting out of debt is never an easy one. For me, it was a process that required hard work, discipline, trust in God, and ultimately a financial miracle. As I reflect on how I went from nearly $200,000 in debt to a position of financial freedom, I see how crucial it was for me to develop new habits, trust in God's provision, and take action toward financial stewardship.

When I first started my financial journey, I was newly married and adjusting to becoming a stepdad. I was excited to begin this new chapter of life, but I had to face some hard truths about my finances. Over the years, I had accumulated close to $200,000 in debt, much of it from reckless spending. I spent the majority of my money on new cars, eating out excessively, movies, and other forms of entertainment that provided short-term gratification but no lasting value. I wasn't thinking about the long-term consequences, and as a result, I found myself buried in debt.

However, the arrival of marriage and becoming a stepdad forced me to rethink my choices. I could no longer afford to live the way I had been living. I had to consider not just my future but the future of my family. The weight of my debt was heavy, and I knew I had to make significant changes in my financial habits if I was going to be a responsible husband, stepdad, and provider.

I didn't have all the answers, but I knew the first step was to trust God for provision. I began praying for wisdom, guidance, and the discipline to make lasting changes. Through prayer and reflection, I began to take concrete steps to get my finances in order. I committed to paying off my debts and set out on a course in financial discipline, even when it felt overwhelming.

Over time, through intentional budgeting, cutting back on unnecessary spending, and adopting wise financial habits, I was able to pay off nearly $80,000 in debt. It was a tough journey, but I began to see progress, and the sense of relief from paying off that portion of debt was immeasurable. By the time I became debt-free, I had learned the value of living within my means and the importance of making intentional choices with my money.

While I was still celebrating the victory of becoming debt-free, a remarkable thing happened. A lawsuit was brought against the schools I had attended, and as a result, my student loans, which had been one of the largest sources of my debt, were completely wiped out. While I wasn't personally involved in the lawsuit, it was a miraculous turn of events that I could not have orchestrated on my own. The lawsuit against the schools resulted in the complete forgiveness of my student loans—a significant portion of my debt—giving me a financial miracle I hadn't anticipated.

Even though the miracle of having my student loans wiped out was a blessing, I realized that I couldn't rely solely on miracles for my financial future. I had already paid off nearly $80,000 through hard work and discipline, and I knew that the remaining journey required continued intentional action. The miracle didn't remove the need for ongoing financial stewardship. I still had to manage my finances wisely and continue making disciplined choices.

This process taught me that true financial freedom comes not from expecting miraculous solutions, but from consistently applying God's principles to how we manage our resources. It was through trusting God for provision, sticking to a plan, and developing new habits that I was able to experience both the miracle and the victory of becoming debt-free.

This devotional journey is a reflection of the principles that helped me break free from financial bondage. It combines biblical wisdom with practical steps for getting out of debt, managing money well, and cultivating financial habits that honor God. Whether you're deep in debt or simply looking to become a better steward of your resources, I hope this guide can help you on your own journey toward financial freedom.

By trusting in God's provision, developing discipline, and applying biblical wisdom, you can experience the same transformation I did. You, too, can become debt-free, find peace in your finances, and honor God with the resources He has entrusted to you.

Examples given throughout the devotionals are fictional but meant to demonstrate the theme.

Stewardship Revolution: 30 Days to Take Control of Your Finances God's Way

Day 1: God Owns it All

"The earth is the Lord's, and all its fullness, the world and those who dwell therein." – Psalm 24:1 (NKJV)

Everything we have belongs to God. From the breath in our lungs to the food on our tables, our homes, our possessions, and even the work we do—none of it is truly ours. Psalm 24:1 makes this clear: the earth and everything in it belongs to God, including us. This truth can be difficult to grasp in a world where we are constantly taught to value ownership and independence. But when we recognize that God is the Creator and ultimate owner of all things, our perspective shifts.

When we understand that everything we have is His, it frees us from the burden of ownership. Instead of feeling the weight of trying to accumulate and protect material possessions, we see ourselves as stewards of the resources God has entrusted to us. Our role is not to hoard or accumulate, but to manage wisely what has been given to us for God's glory. Whether it's our finances, our time, or our talents, all are gifts from God meant to be used in a way that honors Him.

This perspective affects how we view money. For example, when Jane began to see her paycheck as not "hers" but as a gift from God, her approach to finances changed. She no longer made decisions based on personal desires or fears of not having enough. Instead, she prayed about every financial decision, big or small, seeking God's guidance. She realized that God, who owns everything, is also the one who provides for her, and she could trust Him to lead her in how to spend, save, and give. As she prayed and surrendered her financial decisions to God, she experienced greater peace and freedom. The burden of ownership was lifted, and she felt a deep sense of responsibility to manage her resources well, knowing they were not for her own gain but for God's purposes.

Understanding God's ownership of all things also transforms how we live. When we view everything as belonging to Him, we are freed from the tyranny of possessions. We no longer live in a constant state of striving to own more or protect what we have. Instead, we are called to be faithful stewards, using what God has entrusted to us in a way that brings Him glory and advances His Kingdom. As Randy Alcorn puts it, "When we acknowledge that all we have is from God, we begin to live in freedom from the tyranny of possessions." This freedom allows us to use what God has given us to bless others, serve His purposes, and live with an open hand rather than a clenched fist.

Today, take a moment to acknowledge God's ownership over all that you have. In prayer, thank Him for His provision, and ask for wisdom in managing the resources He has entrusted to you. Let go of any sense of ownership over your possessions, knowing that they are temporary gifts meant to be used for God's glory. As you do, may you experience the peace that comes from being a faithful steward of God's resources, living freely in the knowledge that He is the true owner of all.

Alcorn, R. (2002). *The treasure principle: Unlocking the secret of joyfully living God's way*. Multnomah

Day 2: Faithful Stewardship

Matthew 25:14–30

In Matthew 25:14–30, Jesus shares the parable of the talents, a story that highlights the importance of faithful stewardship. A master entrusts three servants with varying amounts of money, expecting them to manage it wisely during his absence. Two of the servants diligently invest and multiply what they've been given, while the third buries his talent out of fear. Upon the master's return, he rewards the two faithful servants for their initiative and responsibility, but the one who buried his talent faces judgment for his inaction. This parable reminds us that God rewards those who manage their resources faithfully, not necessarily based on how much they have, but on how well they use what they've been given.

Faithful stewardship goes beyond mere financial management; it's a reflection of our trust in God and our commitment to His purposes. As Charles Stanley once said, "Stewardship is the commitment of one's self and possessions to God's service." When we recognize that everything we have is ultimately a gift from God, we begin to see ourselves as managers rather than owners. This perspective shifts how we approach not only our money but also our time, talents, and opportunities. Each resource becomes a tool for furthering God's kingdom and reflecting His glory.

Mike's story offers a practical example of this principle in action. Recognizing wasteful habits in his spending, he began tracking his expenses to identify areas of improvement. This simple yet intentional step allowed him to make better financial decisions, avoiding unnecessary expenses and redirecting funds toward meaningful, God-honoring purposes. Like Mike, we are all called to assess how we use the resources God has entrusted to us and seek ways to maximize their impact.

Today, take time to reflect on how you can be more faithful in managing your resources. Are there areas where fear or complacency has kept you from fully utilizing what God has given you? Consider creating a list of practical steps to better steward your income, assets, and time. Whether it's setting a budget, donating to a cause, or volunteering your talents, every effort counts in the eyes of God.

Faithful stewardship is not about perfection but intentionality. When we choose to manage our resources with wisdom and purpose, we honor God and position ourselves to receive His blessings.

Stanley, C. (2006). *The gift of living generously: A biblical guide to managing money.* Thomas Nelson.

Day 3: Breaking Free from Debt

"The rich rules over the poor, and the borrower is servant to the lender." – Proverbs 22:7 (NKJV)

Proverbs 22:7 reminds us that debt has a unique power to enslave, limiting our freedom and weighing us down both spiritually and emotionally. Though debt itself is not a sin, it can dominate our lives, pulling our attention away from serving God and others. When financial obligations consume us, our focus shifts from generosity and purpose to survival and repayment.

Dave Ramsey's words emphasize this reality: "Debt is not a sin, but it is dangerous. It makes us slaves to the lender." The danger lies in how debt controls our decisions, dictating where we direct our energy and often robbing us of peace. Breaking free from debt is not just a financial challenge but a spiritual journey requiring discipline, faith, and trust in God's provision.

Sarah's story shows how small victories can lead to big changes. She started by paying off her smallest debt, gaining momentum with each success. This method, often called the "debt snowball," builds confidence and encourages perseverance. What once felt overwhelming became manageable, and Sarah eventually freed herself from the bondage of debt, opening doors to greater financial and spiritual freedom.

Consider what debts weigh you down spiritually or emotionally. Are there financial burdens, such as credit card balances or loans, that dominate your thoughts? Beyond money, are there emotional or spiritual debts—guilt, regret, or unresolved conflicts—that drain your energy? Recognizing these burdens is the first step toward breaking free.

Today, take a practical step: write down all your debts. While this may feel daunting, it's a powerful act of acknowledgment and accountability. Once listed, commit to a repayment plan. Whether you start with the smallest debt (debt snowball method) like Sarah or focus on those with the highest interest (debt avalanche method), take that first step in faith. Ask God for wisdom and strength to persevere, knowing He desires your freedom.

Breaking free from debt isn't just about financial stability—it's about living the abundant life God intends for you. As you shed the weight of debt, you'll find new opportunities to serve, give, and grow spiritually. Trust in His provision and take each step with faith, knowing that true freedom is possible.

Ramsey, D. (2002). *The total money makeover: A proven plan for financial fitness*. Thomas Nelson.

Day 4: The Danger of Loving Money

"For the love of money is a root of all kinds of evil, for which some have strayed from the faith in their greediness and pierced themselves through with many sorrows." – 1 Timothy 6:10 (NKJV)

In 1 Timothy 6:10, Paul warns that the love of money is a powerful and dangerous force. It is not money itself that causes harm, but the inordinate affection for it—the desire to accumulate wealth at the expense of spiritual health, relationships, and moral integrity. This misplaced love can lead to spiritual ruin, pulling people away from their faith and filling their lives with sorrow.

Randy Alcorn captures this tension perfectly: "You cannot serve God and Money. But you can serve God with money." The distinction lies in whether money is our master or our servant. When we idolize wealth, we risk losing sight of God's purpose for our lives, letting greed dictate our choices. However, when we view money as a tool for serving God, we position ourselves to live with generosity, humility, and joy.

John's story is a vivid illustration of this danger. Driven by the desire for financial security, he began working excessive overtime, believing it would provide a better life for his family. Yet, over time, he realized his obsession with earning more was costing him something far greater: his family's well-being and his own spiritual growth. By recognizing that money had become an idol, John was able to recalibrate his priorities, placing God and his family above his financial ambitions.

Take a moment to reflect on your own attitude toward money. How does it align with biblical values? Are there areas where money may have taken a higher priority than it should? Perhaps it's in the pursuit of wealth, material possessions, or the security that comes from a well-padded bank account. These pursuits, while not inherently wrong, can become dangerous when they overshadow our devotion to God.

Today's action step is to identify areas in your life where money may have become an idol. Be honest with yourself about the ways it influences your decisions, relationships, and spiritual growth. Surrender these areas to God, asking for His guidance in transforming your perspective on wealth.

The danger of loving money is real, but so is the opportunity to use it for God's glory. When we release our grip on wealth and trust God as our provider, we experience true freedom. By serving God with our resources, we align our hearts with His will, finding peace, purpose, and lasting joy.

Alcorn, R. (2002). *The treasure principle: Unlocking the secret of joyfully living God's way*. Multnomah.

Day 5: Contentment in Christ

"Not that I speak in regard to need, for I have learned in whatever state I am, to be content: I know how to be abased, and I know how to abound. Everywhere and in all things I have learned both to be full and to be hungry, both to abound and to suffer need. I can do all things through Christ who strengthens me." – Philippians 4:11–13 (NKJV)

In Philippians 4:11–13, Paul shares a powerful secret: true contentment is not tied to our circumstances but to our relationship with Christ. Whether in abundance or lack, Paul had learned to be content because his strength came from Christ, not from material possessions. This type of contentment is a profound trust in God's provision and sufficiency, allowing us to find peace regardless of our financial or personal situation.

Elisabeth Elliot once said, "Godliness with contentment is great gain. Contentment is learned when we find our satisfaction in Christ alone." Her words remind us that contentment is not something we naturally possess—it's something we cultivate through faith and dependence on God. When we focus on Christ, we stop chasing after the world's fleeting promises of happiness and start experiencing the lasting joy found in Him.

Lisa's journey toward contentment is a beautiful example. She often worried about her finances, feeling anxious and overwhelmed by her needs. One day, she decided to shift her perspective by focusing on gratitude. Instead of fixating on what she lacked, she began thanking God for her health, her supportive relationships, and the small blessings in her daily life. This intentional practice transformed her outlook, helping her find peace in the present rather than striving for more.

Reflect on your own life: where do you struggle with contentment? Perhaps it's in your career, finances, or personal achievements. Are you comparing yourself to others or measuring your worth by what you have rather than who you are in Christ? These struggles can rob us of joy and keep us from fully trusting in God's plan.

Today, take a moment to write a gratitude list focused on non-material blessings. Thank God for things like your relationships, health, spiritual growth, and the beauty of creation. Let this list serve as a reminder that true contentment comes from recognizing His goodness in every season.

Contentment in Christ is a journey of learning to trust Him in all circumstances. By shifting our focus from worldly desires to spiritual fulfillment, we discover a peace that surpasses understanding. Through Christ's strength, we can endure all things and find lasting satisfaction in Him alone.

Elliot, E. (1988). *The path of loneliness: The untold story of Elisabeth Elliot*. Tyndale House.

Day 6: Budgeting with Wisdom

"The plans of the diligent lead surely to plenty, but those of everyone who is hasty, surely to poverty." – Proverbs 21:5 (NKJV)

Proverbs 21:5 highlights the value of careful planning and diligence, especially in financial matters. Budgeting is a practical way to live out this wisdom, requiring intentional effort to allocate resources wisely and avoid impulsive decisions. When we budget thoughtfully, we honor God by managing the blessings He's entrusted to us, ensuring we meet our needs while also preparing for the future.

Charles Swindoll puts it plainly: "Good planning and hard work lead to prosperity, but hasty shortcuts lead to poverty." This truth emphasizes that there are no quick fixes or shortcuts to financial stability. It requires patience, discipline, and commitment to long-term goals. A well-crafted budget not only helps us avoid overspending but also brings clarity and peace, allowing us to live within our means and give generously.

Mark's story demonstrates the power of a disciplined budget. Struggling with overspending, he decided to implement a weekly budgeting system. By breaking down his expenses into manageable portions, he could track where every dollar went and adjust his spending habits. This proactive approach helped him avoid unnecessary expenses, build savings, and reduce financial stress. Mark's diligence paid off, giving him both financial freedom and peace of mind.

Reflect on your current approach to budgeting. Are you diligent and intentional, or do you find yourself reacting to financial pressures without a clear plan? Creating a more realistic budget requires a thorough understanding of your income, expenses, and priorities. It's not just about limiting spending but aligning your financial choices with your values and responsibilities.

Take today's action step: create a budget that accounts for all your monthly expenses. Start by listing your fixed costs, such as rent, utilities, and groceries, and then include discretionary spending like entertainment and dining out. Don't forget to set aside money for savings and giving. Once your budget is in place, review it regularly and adjust as needed.

Budgeting with wisdom is a reflection of our trust in God's provision and our commitment to steward His resources well. By planning diligently and working hard, we position ourselves for financial stability and the ability to bless others. As you take steps to manage your finances wisely, trust that God will guide you and provide for your needs in every season.

Swindoll, C. (2009). *The grace awakening: Believing in grace is one thing. Living it is another.* Zondervan.

Day 7: Trusting God in Your Finances

"Trust in the Lord with all your heart and lean not on your own understanding; in all your ways acknowledge Him, and He shall direct your paths." – Proverbs 3:5–6 (NKJV)

Proverbs 3:5–6 calls us to trust God wholeheartedly, even in areas where we feel most vulnerable—like our finances. Relying on our own understanding can lead to anxiety, poor decisions, and a false sense of control. But when we place our trust in God, we invite Him to lead us on a path of provision and peace. Trusting God with your finances is an act of faith, showing that you believe He is your ultimate provider and guide.

Trusting God means surrendering the need to have everything figured out and allowing Him to work in ways that may not always make sense by human standards. This trust requires humility and a willingness to follow His guidance, even when the path seems uncertain.

Stephanie's journey illustrates the power of trusting God in financial matters. Faced with unexpected expenses and a reduced income, she felt overwhelmed. Yet, instead of relying on her own understanding, she committed her financial situation to God in prayer. She made wise, faith-driven decisions, even when they were difficult. Over time, she witnessed God's provision in surprising ways—whether through unexpected opportunities, the generosity of others, or newfound peace amidst uncertainty.

Consider your own approach: Are you trusting God with your money, or are you relying on your own understanding? Do you find yourself trying to control every financial outcome, or are you willing to seek God's guidance and trust in His plan? Faith in God's provision doesn't mean neglecting responsibility but rather aligning your financial decisions with His will and believing that He will direct your steps.

Today, take a moment to ask God to guide your financial decisions. Whether it's budgeting, saving, giving, or investing, invite Him into every aspect. Pray for wisdom and discernment, trusting that He will provide clarity and direction.

When we trust God with our finances, we experience a deeper sense of peace, knowing that He is in control. Walking in His will allows us to navigate financial challenges with confidence and grace, reminding us that His provision is always enough. As you trust Him with your resources, may you find joy and freedom in knowing that He cares for every detail of your life.

Day 8: Avoiding Impulse Spending

"Whoever has no rule over his own spirit is like a city broken down, without walls." – Proverbs 25:28 (NKJV)

In Proverbs 25:28, Solomon compares a person who lacks self-control to a city without walls—vulnerable and defenseless. Without self-control, our finances are exposed to reckless decisions, and we may fall prey to impulse spending. While we live in a world where consumerism is constant and tempting, learning to manage our finances with discipline and wisdom is essential. Self-control is not just about avoiding spending, but about making intentional choices that honor God and reflect our priorities.

John MacArthur wisely states, "Self-control is the key to living a life that glorifies God in every area, including finances." The ability to control our impulses is a mark of spiritual maturity, showing that we trust God for our needs rather than relying on immediate gratification. By exercising self-control, we choose to live in alignment with our values and avoid being ruled by the desires of the moment.

Jennifer's story offers a practical example of how self-control can change our spending habits. She recognized that shopping was a trigger for impulse buys, often leading to regret and financial strain. To combat this, Jennifer made a simple but powerful change: she began leaving her credit card at home when she went shopping. By removing the immediate access to funds, she gave herself space to think, reflect, and prioritize before making a purchase. This small act of self-discipline helped her avoid unnecessary expenses and brought her peace of mind.

Consider your own spending habits: What triggers your impulse buys? Is it stress, boredom, or the allure of a sale? Identifying these triggers is the first step toward regaining control over your finances. The next step is to commit to a plan that helps you manage those impulses.

Today's action step is to commit to taking 24 hours before making any non-essential purchase. 48 hours is even better. This pause gives you time to consider whether the purchase aligns with your values, whether it's necessary, and whether it will bring lasting satisfaction.

Avoiding impulse spending is an ongoing practice of self-control. By making intentional decisions, we reflect God's wisdom in how we manage our finances. As we build discipline in our spending, we create space to live generously, wisely, and faithfully, bringing glory to God in every area of our lives.

MacArthur, J. (2011). *Self-control: The key to victorious living*. Crossway.

Day 9: Saving for the Future

"Go to the ant, you sluggard! Consider her ways and be wise, which, having no captain, overseer, or ruler, provides her supplies in the summer and gathers her food in the harvest." – Proverbs 6:6–8 (NKJV)

In Proverbs 6:6–8, we are encouraged to look at the ant, a small creature that teaches us an important lesson about preparation and foresight. The ant works diligently in the summer to gather food for the winter, ensuring that it is provided for in times of need. In the same way, we are called to prepare for the future by saving and planning ahead. Whether it's for an emergency, retirement, or other future goals, wise financial planning allows us to face uncertain times with confidence and peace.

Dave Ramsey puts it succinctly: "It's not about how much we make, but how much we save and wisely invest." Saving isn't about accumulating wealth for the sake of wealth; it's about being wise stewards of the resources God has entrusted to us. By saving for the future, we ensure that we can weather unexpected challenges and continue to serve God and others without being burdened by financial stress.

Tom's example is a great illustration of this principle in action. After experiencing a financial setback, he realized that he needed to be more proactive in preparing for future uncertainties. Tom took the step of setting up an emergency fund, which gave him peace of mind during times of financial instability. This small but impactful step not only provided financial security but also gave him the freedom to focus on his goals without the weight of worry.

How are you preparing financially for your future? Are you actively saving, investing, and planning for emergencies or long-term goals? It's easy to overlook future needs when everything seems fine in the present, but as the ant teaches us, preparation is key.

Today's action step is to start a savings account for future goals. This could be an emergency fund, a retirement account, or savings for a specific goal like buying a home or funding education. By setting aside money regularly, you're not only preparing for the future but also building discipline and trust in God's provision.

Saving for the future is an act of wisdom and foresight, allowing us to live in peace and with purpose. Just as the ant prepares for the unknown seasons ahead, we are called to be diligent and faithful stewards of the resources God has entrusted to us, securing a future that aligns with His will.

Ramsey, D. (2002). *The total money makeover: A proven plan for financial fitness*. Thomas Nelson.

Day 10: Giving Generously

"But this I say: He who sows sparingly will also reap sparingly; and he who sows bountifully will also reap bountifully. So let each one give as he purposes in his heart, not grudgingly or of necessity; for God loves a cheerful giver." – 2 Corinthians 9:6–7 (NKJV)

Generosity is more than just a financial transaction; it is a reflection of a heart aligned with God's purposes. In 2 Corinthians 9:6–7, Paul encourages us to give bountifully and cheerfully, not out of obligation but out of a willing and joyful heart. When we give with the right attitude, we participate in God's work, trusting that He will provide for our needs while also blessing others. Generosity is not about how much we give but how we give, and it reveals our trust in God's provision.

However, as we seek to be generous, it's important to use discernment—especially when we are working to get out of debt. Giving should not come at the cost of neglecting our financial responsibilities, such as paying off debt or securing our financial future. It's wise to balance our desire to give with the need to be good stewards of the resources God has entrusted to us. This means being thoughtful about when and how much we give, ensuring that our generosity doesn't lead to financial instability.

David's example highlights how consistent, intentional giving can have a significant impact. He set aside 10% of his income each month for charitable causes, knowing that his generosity would support his community while also keeping him accountable in his financial planning. By prioritizing giving in his budget, David was able to experience the joy of generosity without compromising his financial health.

How do you practice generosity in your life? Are you giving consistently and joyfully, or do you struggle with the balance between generosity and financial responsibility? Reflect on the causes and people you feel called to support and consider how you can give in a way that is both faithful and sustainable.

Today's action step is to find a way to give to a cause that aligns with your values. Whether it's through financial contributions, volunteer work, or other forms of support, make generosity a part of your regular routine. If you are in the process of getting out of debt, consider giving a smaller, manageable amount, trusting that God will honor your willingness to give while you work towards financial freedom.

Generosity is an act of faith and obedience, showing that our hearts are in tune with God's priorities. As we discern the best time and amount to give, we participate in His kingdom work, knowing that He loves a cheerful giver and will provide for our every need.

Stanley, C. (2006). *The gift of living generously: A biblical guide to managing money.* Thomas Nelson.

Day 11: The Power of Prayer in Finances

"Be anxious for nothing, but in everything by prayer and supplication, with thanksgiving, let your requests be made known to God; and the peace of God, which surpasses all understanding, will guard your hearts and minds through Christ Jesus." – Philippians 4:6–7 (NKJV)

In Philippians 4:6–7, we are reminded that prayer should be at the center of all aspects of our lives, including our finances. When faced with financial decisions, uncertainties, or struggles, God invites us to bring our concerns to Him in prayer. Instead of being overwhelmed by anxiety or trying to solve problems in our own strength, we are called to seek God's guidance through prayer, trusting that He will provide us with wisdom and peace.

John Piper reminds us that prayer is not a passive act but an active step of faith, acknowledging our dependence on God in every area of life. "In everything, by prayer and petition, with thanksgiving, present your requests to God." This includes the choices we make about spending, saving, giving, and planning for the future. By inviting God into our financial decisions, we allow Him to lead us, protecting us from poor choices and guiding us toward financial stewardship that honors Him.

Rachel's example demonstrates how powerful prayer can be in making financial decisions. When she received a job offer, she wasn't sure whether it was the right decision for her financially and personally. Rather than rushing into the decision, Rachel prayed for wisdom and discernment. She felt a sense of peace after praying, and God provided the guidance she needed. That job turned out to be a blessing, both financially and in her overall career path. When you are not sure after praying, seek out counsel from other mature believers to assist with discernment.

Do you seek God's guidance when making financial choices? Whether it's a large purchase, investment, career change, or how much to give, God desires to be part of these decisions. Prayer invites Him to guide your steps and provides a sense of peace that transcends worry or doubt.

Today's action step is to set aside time to pray specifically for your finances. Present your concerns to God, whether it's about debt, saving, or career choices. Ask for wisdom and direction, trusting that He will lead you in the way that honors Him.

The power of prayer in our finances is not just about asking for provision but also about aligning our hearts with God's will. As we seek His guidance, He promises to give us peace and wisdom, guarding our hearts from anxiety and leading us toward financial decisions that glorify Him.

Piper, J. (2009). *Don't waste your life*. Crossway.

Day 12: The Blessing of Work

"And whatever you do, do it heartily, as to the Lord and not to men, knowing that from the Lord you will receive the reward of the inheritance; for you serve the Lord Christ." – Colossians 3:23–24 (NKJV)

Work is often viewed simply as a way to earn a living, but in Colossians 3:23–24, Paul shifts our perspective. He teaches us that work is more than just a means of financial gain; it is an opportunity to serve the Lord. Whatever task we undertake, whether it's in the office, at home, or in any other capacity, we are called to do it wholeheartedly, as if we are doing it for God. When we view our work through this lens, it transforms the ordinary into an act of worship.

Tim Keller writes, "Work is not just a job; it's an opportunity to serve God." This powerful reminder helps us see that our daily tasks, no matter how mundane they may seem, are ways to honor God. By approaching work with the mindset that we are serving Him, we not only bring glory to His name but also fulfill His purpose for us—to work for the good of others and to provide for those in need.

For those who are physically unable to work in the traditional sense, it's important to remember that God values every form of service, not just paid employment. Whether through prayer, caring for others, volunteering, or using time and energy in other ways, these efforts are also acts of worship. Your devotion to God, even when physical limitations prevent you from working outside the home, is still an invaluable contribution to His kingdom. Your time spent in prayer, encouragement, or service to others is just as important in God's eyes as any physical labor.

Alex's story demonstrates how a shift in mindset can change the way we approach work. Alex used to view his work simply as a means to pay the bills, but over time, he began to see his job as a way to serve God and provide for his family. This perspective gave him a deeper sense of purpose and fulfillment in his work, even during challenging times. He started to treat every task, no matter how small, as an opportunity to glorify God, whether it was helping a coworker, improving a skill, or simply doing his best each day.

How can you approach your job as a means of serving God? Do you see your work as a platform to bless others, fulfill God's calling, and provide for your needs and the needs of others? If you are physically unable to work, how can you devote your time, energy, and resources to God's work in other ways? Take time to reflect on how your daily efforts can be acts of worship.

Today's action step is to redefine your work as an act of worship. Whether you work inside or outside the home or contribute in different ways, begin to see your efforts as a means to serve God, and ask Him to help you bring excellence and integrity to every task.

Work is a gift from God, and by viewing it through the lens of worship, we fulfill His purpose for our lives and bring honor to His name. Whether through physical labor or other forms of service, our efforts reflect God's love and care, making a lasting impact in His kingdom.

Keller, T. (2012). *Every good endeavor: Connecting your work to God's plan for the world.* Dutton.

Day 13: Handling Financial Temptation

"Do not lay up for yourselves treasures on earth, where moth and rust destroy and where thieves break in and steal; but lay up for yourselves treasures in heaven, where neither moth nor rust destroys and where thieves do not break in and steal. For where your treasure is, there your heart will be also." – Matthew 6:19–21 (NKJV)

In Matthew 6:19–21, Jesus warns us about the dangers of storing up earthly treasures. While it's natural to pursue financial stability and security, our hearts are easily drawn to material wealth. When we focus too much on accumulating possessions or wealth, we can lose sight of God's priorities for our lives. Our hearts tend to follow what we treasure, and if our treasure is in earthly possessions, it can lead us away from the things that truly matter in God's kingdom.

Where is your treasure? Jesus encourages us to invest in things that have eternal value—things like relationships, generosity, and serving others. Earthly treasures are temporary, subject to decay, and easily lost. But when we store up treasures in heaven, we are investing in things that will last forever. This shift in perspective helps guard our hearts against the temptation to prioritize wealth over God's will.

Aubrey's story illustrates how the pursuit of material things can subtly take over our priorities. She realized that her desire for possessions was driving her to overspend, neglecting her long-term financial goals and the things that truly mattered. Once she refocused her attention on eternal priorities—such as being generous, investing in relationships, and supporting causes that aligned with her values—she began to change her spending habits. She recognized that her money could be used as a tool for kingdom purposes rather than for accumulating fleeting treasures.

How can you guard your heart against the temptation to prioritize wealth over God? Take time to evaluate where your money is going and whether it aligns with your values. Are you investing in things that will last, or are you focused on temporary pleasures?

Today's action step is to take a closer look at your spending habits and ensure that your financial choices align with your values. Consider how you can shift your priorities to focus more on storing up treasures in heaven—whether through generosity, investing in relationships, or contributing to causes that reflect God's heart.

As we manage our finances, let's remember that true wealth is found in the things that can never be taken away. By keeping our hearts focused on eternal treasures, we can resist the temptation to place our hope in the fleeting wealth of this world and instead live for what truly matters.

Day 14: God's Provision in Times of Need

"Therefore, do not worry, saying, 'What shall we eat?' or 'What shall we drink?' or 'What shall we wear?' For after all these things the Gentiles seek. For your heavenly Father knows that you need all these things. But seek first the kingdom of God and His righteousness, and all these things shall be added to you." – Matthew 6:31–33 (NKJV)

In Matthew 6:31-33, Jesus reminds us that God knows our needs and will provide for us. When we are faced with financial uncertainty, it's easy to become anxious and worried about how our needs will be met. However, Jesus encourages us to seek God's kingdom and righteousness first, trusting that He will take care of everything else. God is aware of our circumstances and promises to provide for His children in their time of need.

This is not to say that we will always have everything we desire or that provision will come in the way we expect. However, God's provision is faithful, and He provides what we need—often in unexpected ways and at the right time. Austin's story is a testament to this truth. During a period of unemployment, he faced uncertainty and financial strain. Yet, in God's perfect timing, unexpected job opportunities began to arise, allowing Austin to see how God's provision was at work. Even when things seemed bleak, God was faithful to meet David's needs.

Do you trust that God will meet your needs, even in challenging financial times? It can be difficult to let go of worry, but when we choose to focus on God's faithfulness rather than our circumstances, we can experience peace. Reflect on a time when God provided for you unexpectedly. How did He show His faithfulness in your life, and what did you learn from that experience?

Today's action step is to reflect on a time when God provided for you in a way that surprised you. Whether it was a financial blessing, a new opportunity, or an unexpected act of kindness, take time to acknowledge God's provision and thank Him for His faithfulness.

As we trust in God's provision, let's remember that He is faithful to meet our needs. Our job is to seek His kingdom first, knowing that He will add everything we need according to His perfect plan. In times of financial hardship, trust in God's faithfulness and allow Him to guide you through the uncertainty.

Stewardship Revolution: 30 Days to Take Control of Your Finances God's Way

Day 15: Living Below Your Means

"He who is content with little is richer than the one who has much but is always in debt." – Proverbs 13:7 (NKJV)

In Proverbs 13:7, we find wisdom about the value of living within our means. It's easy to fall into the trap of wanting more—whether it's the latest gadget, dining out frequently, or living in a bigger home. However, true contentment isn't found in accumulating more possessions or experiences but in learning to live with what we have. When we choose to live below our means, we free ourselves from the bondage of debt and the anxiety that comes with it. Living within our means requires discipline, self-control, and humility.

The temptation to overspend or keep up with others is strong, but as we see in Proverbs 13:7, contentment with less is actually a form of richness. The person who is satisfied with a simple lifestyle is often more financially free than someone who is constantly pursuing material gain, only to be weighed down by debt. In the context of living God's way, living simply allows us to be more generous, more focused on spiritual growth, and better stewards of the resources He has given us.

In her pursuit of financial freedom, Susan realized that some of her monthly subscriptions and dining habits were taking up more of her budget than necessary. She made the choice to cancel subscription services and cut back on dining out, freeing up more money to save and invest in things that were more aligned with her priorities. By living more simply, she found peace and freedom from the stress that comes with financial strain.

Are there areas in your life where you can cut back on expenses to live more simply? Reflect on your spending habits and consider how living below your means could bring you greater peace, financial freedom, and the ability to give more generously.

Today's action step is to identify a specific area where you can reduce spending in your life. Whether it's canceling unused subscriptions, limiting impulse purchases, or cooking at home more often, choose one area to start cutting back.

Randy Alcorn, in *The Treasure Principle*, writes, "He who is content with little is richer than the one who has much but is always in debt." The pursuit of contentment, not accumulation, is where true wealth lies. By living within our means, we can focus on what truly matters—honoring God, serving others, and enjoying the simple gifts He has already provided.

Alcorn, R. (2002). *The treasure principle: Unlocking the secret of joyfully living God's way*. Multnomah.

Day 16: Avoiding the Love of Money

"For the love of money is the root of all evil, for which some have strayed from the faith in their greediness and pierced themselves through with many sorrows." – 1 Timothy 6:10 (NKJV)

In 1 Timothy 6:9-10, Paul warns us about the dangers of loving money. While money itself is not evil, the love of it can lead us astray, causing us to make poor decisions that harm our spiritual health, relationships, and overall well-being. Money can easily become an idol, something we seek after more than God, and when this happens, we can fall into a pattern of greed and dissatisfaction. The pursuit of wealth can rob us of the peace that comes from contentment in Christ.

Daniel, for example, found himself chasing after a larger paycheck, believing that financial success would bring him happiness and security. However, he soon realized that his constant pursuit of more money was taking a toll on his relationship with God and his family. His spiritual life and family dynamics were suffering because his focus had shifted to material gain. Daniel recognized that he had allowed money to take a higher priority than it should, and he made the necessary adjustments in his life to restore balance and peace.

Have you made any sacrifices in pursuit of wealth that have hurt your spiritual health or relationships? Reflect on whether money has become an idol in your life. Are there areas where you are chasing after financial gain at the expense of your relationship with God or those you love?

Today's action step is to reflect on whether money has taken a higher priority than it should in your life. Consider how the love of money might influence your decisions, relationships, and overall sense of peace.

The pursuit of wealth often promises more than it delivers, but true contentment comes when we find our satisfaction in God, not in material gain. When we choose contentment over the love of money, we align our hearts with God's will and experience a peace that surpasses worldly wealth. Let us choose to treasure what is eternal, investing in relationships, spiritual growth, and generosity, which bring true fulfillment and lasting joy.

Day 17: Financial Peace Through Giving

"It is more blessed to give than to receive." – Acts 20:35 (NKJV)

In Acts 20:35, Paul reminds us that true blessing comes not from receiving, but from giving. It is a powerful truth that can transform our understanding of money and possessions. In a world that encourages us to accumulate wealth and pursue personal gain, the Bible flips this narrative by showing us that generosity brings peace and aligns us with God's will. When we give—whether through finances, time, or talents—we shift our focus from self-centeredness to God's purposes, which brings lasting fulfillment and joy.

Raquel, for example, felt a strong desire to make a difference in her community, so she decided to volunteer at a local food bank. While she expected the experience to be rewarding, she didn't anticipate the peace and joy it would bring to her heart. Through giving her time, Raquel discovered a deeper connection to the needs of others and found that it brought her a sense of contentment and purpose that material possessions could never offer. Her act of service not only impacted the lives of those she helped, but it also gave her a sense of peace that far surpassed any temporary satisfaction from material wealth.

How can you practice giving to others this week? There are countless ways to give, whether through financial support, volunteering, or sharing your skills with those in need. The act of giving allows us to step outside of our own concerns and focus on the well-being of others, which aligns our hearts with God's purposes and brings peace to our lives.

Today's action step is to find an opportunity to give, whether financially or through your time and talents. Whether it's donating to a cause, helping a neighbor, or volunteering your skills, look for ways to give freely, as God has generously given to you.

Dave Ramsey, in *The Total Money Makeover*, teaches that "Financial peace is a result of living within our means and giving generously." When we embrace the principle of giving, we experience a deeper sense of financial peace—not just through our finances, but through the joy and peace that come from living out God's call to love and serve others.

Ramsey, D. (2002). *The total money makeover: A proven plan for financial fitness*. Thomas Nelson.

Day 18: Planning for Financial Security

"Without counsel plans fail, but with many advisers they succeed." – Proverbs 15:22 (NKJV)

Proverbs 15:22 teaches us the importance of wise planning and seeking counsel when making decisions. Financial security doesn't happen by chance; it requires intentional, thoughtful planning. Whether it's saving for the future, investing wisely, or preparing for retirement, planning is a key component in achieving long-term stability. The wisdom found in this verse reminds us that relying on the counsel of others—especially experts—can help ensure that our plans succeed and that we are equipped to handle life's uncertainties.

Jack, for example, realized that in order to secure his family's financial future, he needed a more structured approach to his finances. He sought advice from a financial planner and worked together to create a comprehensive 5-year budget and savings plan. This plan gave him a clear path to follow, which helped him stay focused and disciplined in his spending and saving habits. By making a commitment to long-term financial goals and seeking the right guidance, Jack set himself and his family up for financial success.

Do you have a financial plan in place for the future? If not, today's action step is to begin setting long-term financial goals. Consider what you want to achieve in terms of savings, investing, and retirement, and take practical steps to make those goals a reality. Even if your goals feel distant, taking small, consistent steps now can help you build a secure future.

Charles Swindoll, in *The Grace Awakening*, reminds us that "Wise planning leads to prosperity, while shortcuts or neglect can lead to failure." By being intentional and seeking counsel, we can create a plan that helps us navigate life's financial challenges with confidence and peace. Take the time to invest in your financial future—wisely planned steps today will bring long-term security tomorrow.

Swindoll, C. (2009). *The grace awakening: Believing in grace is one thing. Living it is another.* Zondervan.

Day 19: Debt as a Burden

"The rich rules over the poor, and the borrower is servant to the lender." – Proverbs 22:7 (NKJV)

Debt is more than just a financial obligation—it's a burden that can weigh us down emotionally and spiritually. Proverbs 22:7 clearly shows that borrowing can place us in a position of servitude, where we are controlled by our lenders instead of having the freedom to serve God and others. When we are deeply in debt, it limits our ability to give generously, invest in God's Kingdom, and experience the true financial freedom God desires for us.

Steve experienced this firsthand. He had accumulated credit card debt over the years, and the constant pressure to make payments was affecting his peace of mind and his ability to serve others. But he chose to take control of his finances by starting with the smallest debt first, using the "debt snowball" method. With each debt he paid off, he gained momentum, and the relief of one less obligation motivated him to tackle larger loans.

If you find yourself burdened by debt, today's action step is to start paying off your smallest debts first. This method—though simple—can provide a psychological boost that helps you stay motivated on your journey to becoming debt-free. While it may take time, the financial freedom you gain will allow you to give more, serve others more effectively, and live in the peace that comes from having fewer financial worries.

As Dave Ramsey writes in *The Total Money Makeover*, "Debt is a tool used by the enemy to keep you from living the life you're supposed to live. It ties up your energy, your creativity, and your focus." Debt keeps us in bondage, but by taking steps to pay it off, we reclaim the freedom to live as God intended. Take the first step today and start freeing yourself from the burden of debt.

Ramsey, D. (2002). *The total money makeover: A proven plan for financial fitness*. Thomas Nelson.

Day 20: Honoring God with Your Wealth

"Honor the Lord with your possessions, and with the first fruits of all your increase; so your barns will be filled with plenty, and your vats will overflow with new wine." – Proverbs 3:9-10 (NKJV)

Honoring God with our wealth is about more than giving money—it's about trusting Him with our resources and acknowledging that everything we have comes from Him. Proverbs 3:9-10 reminds us that when we offer God the first and best of what we earn, He promises to bless us abundantly. This act of faith reflects a heart that prioritizes God over material wealth and recognizes Him as the ultimate provider.

Katie's story illustrates this principle beautifully. After much contemplation, she began tithing 10% of her income, even when it felt challenging. She soon discovered that honoring God with her finances brought a sense of peace and purpose that far surpassed any financial gain. Her trust in God deepened, and she felt more content, knowing that her resources were being used for His glory.

When we choose to honor God with our wealth, we acknowledge His sovereignty over our lives. This practice not only blesses others but also strengthens our faith, reminding us that we serve a God who provides for our every need. Setting aside the first portion of our income is a tangible way of expressing our trust in His provision.

As Charles Stanley writes in *The Gift of Living Generously*, "When we give God our first and best, we reflect His goodness and faithfulness in our lives. Our giving becomes a testimony of trust and gratitude." This shift in perspective moves us from merely managing our money to stewarding it in a way that honors God and furthers His Kingdom.

Take a moment today to consider how you can honor God in your financial decisions. Whether it's through tithing, charitable giving, or helping those in need, remember that your act of generosity reflects your trust in God's provision. By prioritizing Him with your wealth, you'll experience the peace and blessings that come from living in alignment with His will.

Stanley, C. (2006). *The gift of living generously: A biblical guide to managing money.* Thomas Nelson.

Day 21: Focusing on Eternal Investments

"Command them to do good, to be rich in good deeds, and to be generous and willing to share. In this way, they will lay up treasure for themselves as a firm foundation for the coming age." – 1 Timothy 6:18-19 (NKJV)

In a world driven by materialism, it's easy to focus on accumulating possessions and wealth. Yet, Scripture reminds us that true riches are found in investing in eternal things. When we give generously, serve others, and use our resources to further God's kingdom, we're building a foundation that lasts beyond this life. Eternal investments are not about the size of the gift but the heart behind it. Every act of kindness, every generous offering, and every moment spent in service points to a higher purpose.

Consider your financial decisions: Are they aligned with eternal values? Do they reflect a heart that prioritizes God's kingdom? Luke, for example, redirected his resources to support missions and found a deeper joy than any material possession could provide. His giving became an act of worship, demonstrating that true wealth isn't in what we keep but in what we give away.

Randy Alcorn puts it well: "What we do with our money shows what we value with our hearts." Our spending habits reveal our priorities, and when those priorities align with God's purposes, we experience peace and fulfillment that surpasses earthly gains.

This week, think about how you can invest in eternity. Whether it's supporting a ministry, volunteering your time, or offering financial help to someone in need, these investments have lasting impact. Trust that God will use your generosity to further His work and multiply your efforts for His glory.

Alcorn, R. (2002). *The treasure principle: Unlocking the secret of joyfully living God's way*. Multnomah.

Day 22: Practicing Patience with Finances

"Therefore, be patient, brethren, until the coming of the Lord. See how the farmer waits for the precious fruit of the earth, waiting patiently for it until it receives the early and latter rain. You also be patient. Establish your hearts, for the coming of the Lord is at hand." – James 5:7-8 (NKJV)

Financial growth, like spiritual growth, often requires patience and trust in God's timing. Just as a farmer waits for the rain to nurture the crops, we must patiently wait for financial blessings to unfold. In our fast-paced world, it's tempting to seek immediate solutions—quick fixes to debt or impulsive investments in hopes of instant returns. However, God often calls us to slow down, trust His process, and learn valuable lessons in the waiting.

Patience allows us to avoid rash decisions that could lead to financial ruin. Instead of taking shortcuts, we can trust in God's timing and seek His guidance for every financial move. Lois's story exemplifies this. She declined several job offers that didn't align with her long-term goals and values. Though waiting was hard, she trusted God's plan, and in His perfect timing, the right opportunity came.

John Piper reminds us: "God is most glorified in us when we are most satisfied in Him." When we find our satisfaction in God rather than material wealth or quick fixes, we reflect His glory in our finances.

Today, reflect on areas where you might need more patience. Are you rushing through financial decisions, or are you waiting on God's direction? Trust that His timing is perfect and that He will guide you toward financial stability and peace when you rely on Him. Stay faithful, stay patient, and know that God is working behind the scenes for your good.

Piper, J. (2009). *Don't waste your life*. Crossway.

Day 23: Living Generously

"Give, and it will be given to you: good measure, pressed down, shaken together, and running over will be put into your bosom. For with the same measure that you use, it will be measured back to you." – Luke 6:38 (NKJV)

Generosity is more than a financial decision; it's a reflection of our faith and trust in God's provision. Jesus' words in Luke 6:38 remind us that when we give with a willing heart, God responds by pouring out blessings in abundance. This verse paints a vivid picture of overflowing blessings, emphasizing that our generosity invites God's generosity in return—not always in material wealth, but often in spiritual richness, joy, and peace.

Living generously doesn't mean giving only when we have extra; it means prioritizing others even when it requires sacrifice. It's about shifting our mindset from scarcity to abundance, trusting that God will supply all our needs as we open our hearts and hands to others. Michael's story illustrates this beautifully. He began contributing not just financially to his local church but also through his time and talents. His willingness to serve opened doors to unexpected opportunities where he could make a difference, and he found that his life felt richer and more meaningful.

Generosity extends beyond financial giving. It includes offering our time, talents, and compassion. Sometimes, the greatest gifts we can offer are intangible—listening to someone in need, offering encouragement, or using our skills to help others. These acts of kindness reflect God's love and can have a ripple effect far beyond what we can see.

Charles Stanley said, "Generosity demonstrates our trust in God. By giving freely, we acknowledge that everything we have comes from Him, and we trust Him to replenish what we give away." This perspective shifts our focus from holding tightly to what we have, to being stewards who manage God's resources with an open hand.

Take a moment today to consider how you can live more generously. Is there someone in need you can bless with your time, resources, or talents? Ask God to reveal opportunities for you to serve others and trust that as you give, He will meet your needs. Living generously is a journey of faith, one that brings us closer to God and allows us to participate in His work of blessing others.

Stanley, C. (2006). *The gift of living generously: A biblical guide to managing money*. Thomas Nelson.

Day 24: Trusting God with Future Provision

"Therefore, I tell you, do not worry about your life, what you will eat or drink; or about your body, what you will wear... Your heavenly Father knows that you need them." – Matthew 6:25, 32

Jesus' teaching in Matthew 6:25-34 invites us to release our anxieties about the future and rest in God's faithfulness. Worrying about tomorrow's needs can consume us, yet Jesus reminds us that our Heavenly Father is fully aware of what we require. Trusting in His provision means placing our future in His hands, believing that He will meet our needs in His perfect timing.

In this passage, Jesus uses nature as an example of God's care: the birds are fed, and the flowers are clothed in beauty, yet they do not toil or worry. If God cares so much for creation, how much more will He care for us? This truth challenges us to shift our focus from anxiety about our future to faith in His provision.

Laura's story is a powerful illustration of this trust. She spent years anxious about her retirement savings, fearing she wouldn't have enough. When she finally surrendered her worries to God through prayer, she experienced a profound sense of peace. Trusting in God didn't eliminate her responsibility to save, but it freed her from the constant fear of insufficiency. She discovered that faith in God's provision brought clarity to her financial planning and peace to her heart.

John Piper emphasizes this faith in *Don't Waste Your Life*, saying, "God is most glorified in us when we are most satisfied in Him." When we trust God to provide, we demonstrate our satisfaction in His sovereignty and goodness rather than relying solely on our efforts. This trust glorifies God and deepens our relationship with Him.

If you find yourself worrying about your future, take today's action step: write down your concerns and present them to God in prayer. Whether it's retirement, health, or job security, surrender your fears and ask Him to guide you. Trusting God doesn't mean we ignore our responsibilities, but it shifts the burden of worry from us to Him.

As you trust God for future provision, remember His faithfulness in the past. Let His care for you today strengthen your confidence in tomorrow. Trusting God with your future is a daily act of faith, but it leads to a life of peace and reliance on His unwavering provision.

Piper, J. (2009). *Don't waste your life*. Crossway.

Day 25: The Power of Contentment

"I can do all things through Christ who strengthens me." – Philippians 4:13

Contentment is often misunderstood as something that will come once we have all our desires fulfilled. However, Paul's words in Philippians 4:11-13 challenge this misconception. True contentment doesn't depend on our circumstances or what we possess—it depends on our reliance on Christ's strength in all situations. Whether in abundance or need, contentment comes when we learn to be satisfied with what God has given us and trust that He will provide for our needs.

Paul, who had experienced both riches and poverty, understood the secret of contentment. He was not swayed by his changing circumstances but was grounded in the strength of Christ. This lesson teaches us that contentment isn't about having everything we want, but about having peace in knowing that God is enough for us. It's about shifting our focus from longing for more to being thankful for what we have and trusting that God will provide everything we need in His perfect time.

Tom's experience illustrates this well. For years, Tom struggled with comparing his life to others. He often found himself wishing for more—more money, a bigger house, a more luxurious lifestyle. But one day, Tom realized that these comparisons were stealing his peace and joy. He decided to focus on gratitude instead of envy. By reflecting on the blessings he had, like his health, family, and the provision he had received, Tom found his heart shifting toward contentment. Over time, this mindset transformed his perspective, and he was able to enjoy life as it was, without constantly looking for what he didn't have.

John Alcorn, in *The Treasure Principle*, writes, "The secret of contentment is not in getting everything we want, but in trusting that God knows what is best for us and that He will provide accordingly." This powerful insight aligns with the heart of Philippians 4:13—our strength comes not from our circumstances, but from the sufficiency of Christ.

If you're struggling with discontentment, take some time today to reflect on what you have rather than what you lack. Write down things you are thankful for and surrender your desires to God. Ask Him to help you cultivate a heart of contentment, finding joy in His provision rather than striving for more. Remember, contentment is not the absence of desires, but the peace that comes when we trust that God is enough.

Alcorn, R. (2002). *The Treasure Principle: Unlocking the Secret of Joyfully Living God's Way*. Multnomah.

Day 26: The Role of Saving

"The wise store up choice food and olive oil, but fools gulp theirs down." – Proverbs 21:20

In Proverbs 21:20, we find a simple yet profound lesson: wise individuals prioritize saving for the future, while the foolish live only for the present, neglecting to prepare for what lies ahead. This verse highlights the importance of saving and being diligent stewards of the resources God has given us. Saving is not just about accumulating wealth; it's about exercising wisdom, being responsible, and creating security for the future, especially in times of uncertainty or unexpected expenses.

God calls us to be wise with our finances, and one of the key aspects of wise financial management is saving. A savings plan allows us to meet our future needs without relying on debt. Whether it's for emergencies, future purchases, or retirement, having savings in place can give us peace of mind and enable us to honor God with our financial decisions.

Stephanie's story is a great example of this principle in action. Early in her financial journey, she realized that living paycheck to paycheck wasn't sustainable, so she made the decision to begin saving a small percentage of her income each month. Over time, Stephanie built a solid emergency fund, which gave her peace of mind when unexpected expenses arose. She no longer felt the stress of financial uncertainty because she had taken the proactive step to prepare for the future.

Dave Ramsey, in *The Total Money Makeover*, writes, "The key to building wealth is a plan, and the first step in that plan is saving." His advice aligns with the biblical principle of preparing for the future and securing what God has entrusted to us. Saving doesn't mean hoarding wealth for selfish gain, but it's about being prepared and setting aside resources to handle life's challenges and opportunities.

If you don't already have a savings plan, take today's action step and begin one. Start small if necessary but be consistent. Set a goal for your savings, whether it's building an emergency fund or saving for a specific financial need. Trust that as you steward your finances well, God will guide and provide for you in the future.

Remember, saving is an act of faith—it shows that we trust in God's provision and are willing to plan for the future with wisdom.

Ramsey, D. (2002). *The Total Money Makeover: A Proven Plan for Financial Fitness*. Thomas Nelson.

Day 27: Generosity and Blessing Others

"God loves a cheerful giver." – 2 Corinthians 9:7

In 2 Corinthians 9:6-7, Paul reminds us that generosity is not just about giving but about the attitude in which we give. God's heart is moved by a cheerful giver, someone who gives willingly and joyfully, not out of obligation. When we approach giving with a spirit of generosity, we open ourselves to experience the abundance of God's blessings. Giving is an act of worship, aligning our hearts with God's desires and acknowledging that all we have is a gift from Him.

Generosity doesn't only impact the recipient, but it also transforms the giver. Jesus modeled this in His life, showing us that our giving, whether financial or through our time, talents, or love, can reflect the heart of God. Paul encourages us that when we give, we are sowing seeds for a harvest of righteousness—not just for others, but for ourselves too. Generosity breaks the grip of materialism and teaches us to rely on God rather than wealth.

Mick's journey with generosity illustrates the power of giving. He initially contributed to a local food pantry because he felt it was the right thing to do. Over time, however, as he saw the difference his giving made, he found that it brought him joy and a deep sense of purpose. His perspective shifted from giving out of duty to giving as an expression of love. He discovered that the more he gave, the more his heart opened to God's work in his life, and he was blessed in ways he didn't expect.

Chuck Swindoll emphasizes in *The Grace Awakening* that "Believing in grace is one thing. Living it is another." Generosity is a practical outpouring of the grace we've received from God. When we live with open hands, ready to bless others, we become conduits of His love and provision.

As you reflect on today's verse, think about how you can live generously. Your act of kindness or giving doesn't have to be large. Whether you contribute financially, give of your time, or simply offer a listening ear, today is an opportunity to bless someone in need. Remember, God loves a cheerful giver, and through our generosity, we are partners in God's work in the world.

Swindoll, C. (2009). *The Grace Awakening: Believing in Grace Is One Thing. Living It Is Another.* Zondervan.

Day 28: Seeking God's Guidance in Financial Decisions

"If any of you lacks wisdom, let him ask of God, who gives to all liberally and without reproach." – James 1:5

When making significant financial decisions, it is essential to seek God's wisdom. James 1:5 reminds us that God offers wisdom generously to those who ask. Financial decisions can often feel overwhelming—whether it's purchasing a new car, making an investment, or planning for retirement—but God is ready to guide us. By turning to Him in prayer, we acknowledge that His understanding surpasses our own and that His plans for us are greater than anything we could imagine.

When we seek God's wisdom, we are not simply looking for a way to make decisions that benefit us personally, but we are also aligning ourselves with His will. As Proverbs 3:5-6 teaches, we are to trust in the Lord with all our hearts and lean not on our understanding, acknowledging Him in all our ways. This means that financial decisions are not just about numbers; they are also about trusting God's direction in our lives and His provision.

Naomi's story provides a practical example of this. Naomi had been saving for a new car for several months, but she wanted to be sure that the purchase was in line with God's will. Before making the final decision, she prayed for guidance and felt a deep sense of peace about the car she was choosing. Naomi's decision wasn't just about getting a good deal; it was about trusting God's guidance and being at peace with her choices. This is the kind of wisdom God gives when we ask Him for it—wisdom that leads to peace and confidence in our decisions.

Charles Stanley emphasizes that God is generous with wisdom. He gives it freely to those who seek it. As you consider your next financial decision, remember that God is ready to guide you. Whether it's a small or large decision, take time to pray and ask for His wisdom.

Today's action step: Before making any significant financial decision, take time to pray and seek counsel from God. Ask for wisdom and peace in your heart, trusting that He will guide you to make the best choice.

Stanley, C. (2009). *The Gift of Living Generously: A Biblical Guide to Managing Money.* Thomas Nelson.

Day 29: Overcoming the Trap of Materialism

"Watch out! Be on your guard against all kinds of greed; life does not consist in an abundance of possessions." – Luke 12:15

In Luke 12:15, Jesus warns us against the dangers of greed and materialism. He reminds us that life is not about accumulating possessions but about cultivating a deep relationship with God. While society often measures success by wealth and material goods, Jesus calls us to a different standard. True wealth is found in our connection with God, not in the things we own.

Materialism can subtly take root in our lives, leading us to focus more on acquiring things than on nurturing the relationships and values that matter most. Jesus cautions us to be vigilant against all forms of greed, as they can divert our hearts from what is truly important. The pursuit of wealth can easily become a trap, robbing us of contentment and distracting us from living according to God's purpose.

Becky's story is an example of overcoming materialism. She realized that her large home, full of things she didn't truly need, was taking her focus away from her family and her faith. After careful reflection, Becky decided to downsize her home and simplify her life. She chose to invest more time and energy into relationships with her family, friends, and God. By letting go of the constant desire for more possessions, Becky found greater peace and fulfillment in the things that truly mattered.

Randy Alcorn encourages us to view our possessions as tools to be used for God's kingdom, rather than treasures to hoard for ourselves. He reminds us that generosity and contentment are key to overcoming materialism. When we recognize that everything we have is a gift from God, we are freed from the need to keep accumulating. True wealth is measured by our love for God and others, not by the size of our bank account or the things we own.

Take today's action step: Identify areas in your life where materialism may be taking root. This might involve downsizing, letting go of unnecessary possessions, or refocusing your priorities. Ask God to help you guard your heart against greed and remind you of the true riches that come from a life lived for Him.

Alcorn, R. (2002). *The Treasure Principle: Unlocking the Secret of Joyfully Living God's Way*. Multnomah.

Day 30: Faithful Stewardship of All Resources

"Each of you should use whatever gift you have received to serve others, as faithful stewards of God's grace." – 1 Peter 4:10

In 1 Peter 4:10, we are reminded that as stewards of God's grace, we are called to manage all the resources He has entrusted to us—time, talents, and finances—in a way that honors Him. Stewardship goes beyond just financial management; it encompasses every area of our lives. God has blessed each of us with unique gifts and resources, and we are responsible for using them wisely and for His glory.

This concept of stewardship challenges us to view everything we have—our money, our time, our abilities—not as our own, but as gifts given by God to be used for His purposes. When we are faithful stewards, we recognize that our resources are tools for advancing His kingdom, not for self-indulgence or accumulation. Every decision we make with our time and money should reflect a heart that desires to honor God and serve others.

Carlos is an example of faithful stewardship. He recognized that his financial knowledge could be used to help others. So, he began volunteering his expertise to assist people in building better budgets and creating sustainable financial plans. By offering his talents for the benefit of others, Carlos not only helped individuals improve their financial situations but also fulfilled his calling to be a faithful steward of God's grace. His willingness to use his resources for the good of others advanced God's kingdom and deepened his own relationship with God.

Charles Swindoll, in *The Grace Awakening*, reminds us that grace isn't just about receiving; it's about living it out. As stewards of God's grace, we are called to live in a way that reflects His generosity. Our financial decisions, how we manage our time, and how we use our talents should all be driven by a desire to serve God and others.

As you reflect on today's devotion, take time to evaluate how you are using your financial resources to advance God's kingdom. Are there areas where you can improve? Consider how you can be a better steward of the gifts and resources God has given you. Ask Him to guide your decisions and be open to new opportunities to serve others through your time and finances.

Swindoll, C. (2009). *The Grace Awakening: Believing in Grace Is One Thing. Living It Is Another.* Zondervan.

Day 31 (Bonus Devotional): The Reward of Faithful Stewardship

"Well done, good and faithful servant; you have been faithful over a little; I will set you over much. Enter into the joy of your master." – Matthew 25:23

Stewardship is not just about managing our finances; it's about being faithful in every area of our lives. In Matthew 25:14-30, Jesus shares the parable of the talents, showing us that God entrusts us with different resources—whether time, talents, or treasure—and calls us to manage them wisely. The reward for faithful stewardship is not just financial success, but a deeper relationship with God and an eternal reward. God has entrusted us with the resources we have, and how we manage them reflects our trust in His provision and purpose. This is why we must seek His guidance in our financial decisions, practice generosity, and stay committed to saving for the future.

We are stewards of everything God has given us, and being faithful in managing these resources brings us joy both in the present and in the future. As Christians, we are called to honor God with our resources, knowing that our faithfulness will lead to rewards, both on earth and in heaven.

God does not measure success by the amount we accumulate but by the faithfulness and heart we demonstrate in managing what He's given us. The beauty of this principle is that when we honor God with our finances, we experience the joy of participating in His work and growing closer to Him.

Reflection is essential here. How are you managing the resources God has entrusted to you? Are you faithful with your time, money, and abilities? What steps can you take today to be more faithful in your stewardship? Take a moment to reflect on the areas of your life where you may need to improve your stewardship. Commit to making a plan to be more intentional with your time, money, and talents. Ask God for wisdom and strength as you seek to honor Him with what He has given you.

John had always struggled with his finances, but after committing to being a faithful steward, he started creating a budget, saving for the future, and being more generous. Over time, John not only saw his financial situation improve, but he also experienced greater peace and joy in knowing he was honoring God with his resources. "Well done, good and faithful servant; you have been faithful over a little; I will set you over much." – Matthew 25:23.

May we, too, hear these words from our Heavenly Father as we manage the gifts He has entrusted to us, for His glory.

Conclusion:

The journey to financial freedom is a process that requires hard work, discipline, and trust in God. The principles I've shared are grounded in biblical stewardship, which has been the foundation of the habits that helped me pay off nearly $200,000 in debt. It's essential to understand that while God is capable of performing miracles, He also calls us to be diligent stewards of the resources He has entrusted to us. As Christians, we are not only called to manage our finances wisely but also to be generous with what we have, reflecting Christ's love and generosity to others. Our financial practices should show the world that we serve a generous God, and through our giving, others may see Christ in us.

Getting out of debt is not a quick fix but rather a commitment to change—change in how we manage our money and align our financial practices with God's Word. This journey requires personal responsibility, consistent action, and unwavering faith in God's provision. It's a daily act of trust in Him, knowing that He is faithful to provide for our needs and guide us toward financial freedom.

This process takes time, effort, and trust in God's timing to see lasting results. With Him, all things are possible. Through His wisdom, we can become faithful stewards of the resources He has given us. We are called to manage not just for ourselves, but also to share generously so that others may see the reflection of His love in our actions. I hope these principles will guide you toward a healthier financial future, but always remember, the journey to financial freedom is not just about numbers—it's about trusting God with every aspect of our lives, including our resources.

Outline of Debt Payment Methods and Saving Methods

Debt Payment Methods

1. **Debt Snowball Method**
    - **Description:** Focus on paying off the smallest debt first while making minimum payments on others. Once the smallest debt is paid off, move to the next smallest, using the money you were putting toward the first debt.
    - **Advantages:** Builds momentum and motivation by quickly eliminating smaller debts.
    - **Disadvantages:** May result in paying more interest over time since higher-interest debts are paid off later.
    - **Best for:** Individuals who need motivation and prefer quick wins.
2. **Debt Avalanche Method**
    - **Description:** Focus on paying off the debt with the highest interest rate first while making minimum payments on others. Once the highest-interest debt is paid off, move to the next highest.
    - **Advantages:** Saves money on interest over the long term, as higher-interest debts are eliminated first.
    - **Disadvantages:** May take longer to pay off a debt, which could be discouraging for some.
    - **Best for:** Individuals who are highly motivated by saving money and focusing on the most cost-effective strategy.
3. **Debt Consolidation**
    - **Description:** Combine multiple debts into one loan with a lower interest rate or easier terms (e.g., a personal loan or a balance transfer credit card).
    - **Advantages:** Simplifies payments and may reduce interest rates or fees.
    - **Disadvantages:** May involve fees or require collateral; doesn't address underlying financial habits.
    - **Best for:** People with multiple debts who want simplicity and potentially lower interest.
4. **Debt Settlement**
    - **Description:** Negotiate with creditors to settle debts for less than what is owed, often through a third-party debt settlement company.
    - **Advantages:** Potentially reduces the total debt.
    - **Disadvantages:** Can negatively affect credit scores; may involve fees; may not be available for all types of debt.
    - **Best for:** Individuals struggling with significant debt and seeking a way to resolve it quicker.
5. **Debt Management Plan (DMP)**
    - **Description:** Work with a credit counseling agency to create a structured payment plan that consolidates monthly payments into one lower payment, often with negotiated interest reductions.
    - **Advantages:** Streamlines payments, often with lower interest rates, and provides professional guidance.

- **Disadvantages:** May involve fees, and the plan may take several years to complete.
- **Best for:** People looking for a structured, professional approach to resolving debt with guidance.
6. **Bankruptcy**
    - **Description:** A legal process to eliminate or restructure debt. Depending on the type of bankruptcy, some debts are discharged, while others are reorganized.
    - **Advantages:** Offers relief from debt and stops collections.
    - **Disadvantages:** Severe impact on credit; long-term effects on financial health.
    - **Best for:** Individuals with overwhelming debt who have no other viable options.

Saving Methods

1. **Emergency Fund Savings**
    - **Description:** Set aside money for unexpected expenses, such as medical bills, car repairs, or job loss. The goal is typically 3-6 months of living expenses.
    - **Advantages:** Provides financial security in case of emergencies, reducing the need for debt.
    - **Disadvantages:** May take time to build, especially when living paycheck to paycheck.
    - **Best for:** Everyone, as an emergency fund is foundational to financial security.
2. **High-Yield Savings Account**
    - **Description:** A savings account that offers a higher interest rate than a regular savings account, helping money grow faster.
    - **Advantages:** Higher interest rate, easy access to funds, low-risk.
    - **Disadvantages:** Limited withdrawal frequency or minimum balance requirements.
    - **Best for:** People looking to save for mid-term goals, such as an emergency fund or a large purchase.
3. **Certificate of Deposit (CD)**
    - **Description:** A savings account with a fixed interest rate and a fixed term, usually ranging from a few months to several years.
    - **Advantages:** Higher interest rates than savings accounts, guaranteed return.
    - **Disadvantages:** Penalty for early withdrawal; less flexibility in accessing funds.
    - **Best for:** Individuals who can lock away their savings for a set period and want a guaranteed return.
4. **Automatic Savings Plans**
    - **Description:** Set up automatic transfers from your checking account to your savings account, so you regularly save a portion of your income.
    - **Advantages:** Makes saving effortless and consistent, removes the temptation to spend.
    - **Disadvantages:** Requires careful budgeting to ensure enough funds remain in your checking account for regular expenses.
    - **Best for:** Those who struggle with saving or tend to spend most of their income.

5. **Retirement Accounts (401(k), IRA, Roth IRA)**
   - **Description:** Contribute a portion of your income to retirement accounts, such as a 401(k), traditional IRA, or Roth IRA. These accounts offer tax benefits.
   - **Advantages:** Long-term growth, tax-deferred or tax-free growth depending on the account type.
   - **Disadvantages:** Withdrawal penalties before retirement age, limits on annual contributions.
   - **Best for:** Anyone looking to plan for long-term financial security and retirement.
6. **Investment Accounts**
   - **Description:** Invest money in stocks, bonds, or mutual funds to grow wealth over time.
   - **Advantages:** Potential for higher returns than savings accounts or CDs.
   - **Disadvantages:** Risk of losing money; requires knowledge and attention to market conditions.
   - **Best for:** Individuals with a long-term horizon and the ability to take on some investment risk.
7. **Cash-Envelope System**
   - **Description:** Allocate a specific amount of cash for categories like groceries, entertainment, and transportation. When the cash runs out, no more spending is allowed in that category.
   - **Advantages:** Helps with budgeting and controlling spending; tangible way to manage money.
   - **Disadvantages:** Less convenient in an increasingly digital world; can be hard to stick to.
   - **Best for:** People who need a physical, structured approach to limit spending.
8. **Zero-Based Budgeting**
   - **Description:** Plan every dollar of your income, giving each dollar a specific job (whether it's saving, spending, or giving).
   - **Advantages:** Encourages intentional saving and financial awareness.
   - **Disadvantages:** Requires meticulous planning and constant tracking.
   - **Best for:** People looking for a detailed, organized approach to budgeting and saving.
9. **Debt-Specific Savings (for Paying Down Debt)**
   - **Description:** Save for paying off specific debts (e.g., credit card or student loans) by allocating funds that would otherwise go into savings or investment accounts.
   - **Advantages:** Helps target and eliminate debt more quickly, preventing interest from growing.
   - **Disadvantages:** Delays other savings goals.
   - **Best for:** Individuals focused on debt reduction before saving for other goals.

List of Resources for Budgeting Apps and Other Financial Resources

Budgeting Apps

1. **Mint**
    - **Description:** Mint is a free budgeting app that tracks expenses, creates a budget, and helps with bill payments. It syncs with your bank accounts, credit cards, and investments.
    - **Key Features:** Budgeting tools, bill tracking, credit score monitoring, financial goals.
    - **Best For:** Beginners looking for a free, easy-to-use app that helps track expenses and manage money.
2. **YNAB (You Need A Budget)**
    - **Description:** YNAB is a paid budgeting app that uses the zero-based budgeting method. It helps you prioritize your spending and save money based on your goals.
    - **Key Features:** Goal-setting, expense tracking, zero-based budgeting system, financial education resources.
    - **Best For:** Those who want a more hands-on, proactive budgeting system with educational support.
3. **EveryDollar**
    - **Description:** Created by financial expert Dave Ramsey, EveryDollar is a budgeting tool that helps users follow the zero-based budgeting method.
    - **Key Features:** Simple interface, financial tracking, budget templates, integration with bank accounts (premium version).
    - **Best For:** Users who are following Dave Ramsey's Baby Steps program and want a straightforward, easy-to-use tool.
4. **GoodBudget**
    - **Description:** GoodBudget is a digital envelope system that allows you to plan and track your spending by dividing your income into envelopes for different categories.
    - **Key Features:** Envelope budgeting, debt tracking, savings goals, syncs across devices.
    - **Best For:** Those who prefer a cash-envelope method and want a simple, accessible app for family or group budgeting.
5. **PocketGuard**
    - **Description:** PocketGuard helps track your spending and find opportunities to save. It links to bank accounts and automatically categorizes transactions.
    - **Key Features:** Spending limits, savings goals, transaction categorization, subscription tracking.
    - **Best For:** People who want to easily monitor their spending and see how much money they have left to spend after bills and savings.
6. **Clarity Money**
    - **Description:** Clarity Money helps users track spending, set budgets, and find ways to save. It also provides recommendations for better financial habits.

- **Key Features:** Bill tracking, savings recommendations, subscription cancellation, budgeting tools.
- **Best For:** Users looking for an easy-to-use app that offers helpful tips to cut costs and save.

7. **Simple (formerly known as Simple Bank)**
   - **Description:** Simple offers a mobile banking service with built-in budgeting features, such as Goals, which lets users set savings objectives and track progress.
   - **Key Features:** Budgeting, savings goals, expense tracking, automatic savings features.
   - **Best For:** People who want an all-in-one mobile banking and budgeting solution.

8. **Personal Capital**
   - **Description:** Personal Capital combines budgeting with investment tracking. It provides tools for budgeting while giving you a full picture of your financial health, including assets and liabilities.
   - **Key Features:** Net worth tracking, investment tracking, retirement planning tools, budgeting.
   - **Best For:** Individuals who want to manage both their day-to-day budget and long-term financial goals.

9. **Zeta**
   - **Description:** Zeta is designed for couples to manage finances together. It includes shared expense tracking, bill reminders, and budgeting tools.
   - **Key Features:** Shared budget, bill tracking, goal setting, category tracking.
   - **Best For:** Couples or families managing finances together.

Other Financial Resources

1. **Dave Ramsey's Financial Peace University**
   - **Description:** A comprehensive course designed to help individuals and families get out of debt, build savings, and live financially free. It includes step-by-step instructions for budgeting, saving, and paying off debt.
   - **Key Features:** Video lessons, worksheets, budgeting tools, debt-free plan.
   - **Best For:** People committed to following the Baby Steps and learning financial principles grounded in biblical stewardship.

2. **The Financial Diet**
   - **Description:** An online resource offering financial education, budgeting advice, and tips for managing personal finances, especially geared toward women.
   - **Key Features:** Budgeting tips, personal finance blogs, interviews with financial experts, resources for side hustles.
   - **Best For:** Women looking for financial tips and advice on budgeting, saving, and building wealth.

3. **You Need A Budget (YNAB) Blog & Resources**
   - **Description:** YNAB offers a wealth of free financial education through its blog, guides, and resources, which help users learn how to manage money and budget effectively.

- **Key Features:** Articles, financial guides, workshops, free budgeting resources.
- **Best For:** Those using YNAB or anyone looking to learn more about proactive budgeting and personal finance.

4. **National Foundation for Credit Counseling (NFCC)**
   - **Description:** The NFCC offers services for debt management, credit counseling, and financial education. It provides both resources and certified counselors to help people manage debt and improve financial habits.
   - **Key Features:** Credit counseling, debt management plans, financial education resources.
   - **Best For:** Individuals who need help with debt management or financial advice from certified professionals.

5. **Khan Academy: Personal Finance**
   - **Description:** A free online resource offering courses on budgeting, saving, investing, and retirement planning. Khan Academy provides high-quality education for free.
   - **Key Features:** Video lessons, exercises, quizzes, and financial topics explained in an easy-to-understand format.
   - **Best For:** Those looking for free, comprehensive financial education.

6. **Smart About Money (by the National Endowment for Financial Education)**
   - **Description:** Smart About Money offers tools, tips, and resources to help people learn about budgeting, managing debt, saving, investing, and more.
   - **Key Features:** Budgeting tools, financial calculators, educational articles, self-assessment tools.
   - **Best For:** People looking to start managing their money with access to free financial planning resources.

7. **Mint Life Blog**
   - **Description:** The Mint Life blog offers financial tips, budgeting advice, and strategies for saving money and managing personal finances, especially in everyday life.
   - **Key Features:** Money management tips, budgeting advice, saving strategies, personal finance guides.
   - **Best For:** Mint users looking for more in-depth financial advice and money-saving strategies.

8. **The Motley Fool**
   - **Description:** A personal finance site that provides investment tips, stock market advice, budgeting tools, and retirement planning guides.
   - **Key Features:** Investment strategies, stock recommendations, personal finance articles, retirement resources.
   - **Best For:** Individuals looking to invest, plan for retirement, or learn more about personal finance.

9. **Broke Millennial**
   - **Description:** A resource aimed at helping millennials navigate their finances, from getting out of debt to budgeting, saving, and investing.
   - **Key Features:** Financial advice for young adults, budgeting strategies, investing guides, student loan tips.
   - **Best For:** Millennials looking for financial advice tailored to their generation.

10. **PocketSmith**
    - **Description:** A personal finance app and software that allows you to track your spending, create budgets, and plan for the future with a cash flow forecasting tool.
    - **Key Features:** Budget tracking, financial forecasting, reports, bill reminders.
    - **Best For:** Users who want to project their finances and see how their spending habits affect future cash flow.